The Kimono of the Geisha-Diva Ichimaru

THE KIMONO
of the Geisha-Diva Ichimaru

BARRY TILL

MICHIKO WARKENTYNE

JUDITH PATT

Pomegranate

SAN FRANCISCO

Published by Pomegranate Communications, Inc.
Box 808022, Petaluma CA 94975
800 227 1428; www.pomegranate.com

Pomegranate Europe Ltd.
Unit 1, Heathcote Business Centre, Hurlbutt Road
Warwick, Warwickshire CV34 6TD, UK
[+44] 0 1926 430111; sales@pomeurope.co.uk

FRONTISPIECE *Portrait of the Geisha Ichimaru,* Kiyoshi Kobayakawa (1898–1948). Hanging scroll,
ink and colors on silk. Gift of Mrs. Fumi Suzuki, AGGV 2001.004.001.

Library of Congress Cataloging-in-Publication Data
Till, Barry, 1951–.
    The kimono of the geisha-diva Ichimaru / Barry Till, Michiko Warkentyne, and Judith Patt.
        p. cm.
    Includes bibliographical references.
    ISBN 0-7649-3513-5 (alk. paper)
        1. Kimonos. 2. Ichimaru. 3. Ichimaru—Clothing. 4. Geishas—Biography. I. Warkentyne, Michiko.
II. Patt, Judith.   III. Title.

GT1560.T54 2006
391—dc2   2005051493

Pomegranate Catalog No. A115

Design by Lynn Bell, Monroe Street Studios, Santa Rosa, California

15 14 13 12 11 10 09 08 07 06   10 9 8 7 6 5 4 3 2 1

CONTENTS

In late 2001, the Art Gallery of Greater Victoria was very fortunate to receive a magnificent collection of *kimono, obi,* jewelry, records, tapes, and other paraphernalia that had belonged to the geisha-diva Ichimaru (1906–1997), from Ichimaru's friend and confidante, Mrs. Fumi Suzuki of Tokyo.

Ichimaru was one of the most famous geisha of twentieth-century Japan. Due to her extraordinary voice, she eventually left the geisha world to become a major singing talent in Japan. She would, however, continue to perform in full geisha regalia throughout her long and illustrious career, and in true geisha fashion would continue to purchase beautiful kimono. These kimono demonstrate her style and taste over several decades.

Before discussing the kimono of Ichimaru, a brief look at the geisha lifestyle and the life and times of Ichimaru will serve to put things in the proper context.

HOMONGI WITH DESIGN DEPICTING KIMONO
HANGING ON ROPES (DETAIL)

In Japan, the occupation of geisha has a long and honorable history. Geisha—high-class, well-educated hostess-courtesans—entertained wealthy, sophisticated, and powerful Japanese men who desired cultured and brilliant conversation and elegant entertainment in an atmosphere of decadent refinement. The geisha profession has lasted so long in Japanese society because it has provided more than just sex—it was an admired art form. In 1956, when the government abolished legal prostitution in Japan, those cultivated ladies, the geisha, were exempted from the law, implying that they should be viewed as exotic entertainers preserving the traditional arts, not as prostitutes.

The geisha tradition goes back to the Edo period (1615–1868) and the world of the Kabuki theater and the pleasure quarters (or "floating world"), separated from the rest of the city by walls, found in the major cities of Edo (Tokyo), Osaka, and Kyoto. By 1779, the government licensed the pleasure quarters and issued a code of professional conduct with disciplinary rules and regulations. The Kabuki theater provided entertainment for the townspeople, and many teahouses were set up nearby for food and drink. The actors and theatergoers who frequented the teahouses, as well as patrons of the brothels within the pleasure quarters, often enlivened their parties by requesting the services of independent performers who could sing, dance, and play music. These performers came to be called *geisha* in the seventeenth century. The word is made up of two characters: *gei*, meaning "art" or "accomplished," and *sha*, "person"—so *geisha* can be translated as "accomplished person" or "person who lives by the arts."

The earliest geisha were male entertainers, jesters, and musicians, but by about 1780, female geisha outnumbered male geisha and soon came to totally dominate the trade. Some of the younger courtesans in the pleasure quarters turned to the role of entertainer. As professional entertainers and hostesses, geisha became an important part of traditional social life for

FROZEN: THE APPEARANCE OF A FUKAGAWA NAKAMICHI GEISHA OF THE TENPO ERA (1830–1844), *Taiso Yoshitoshi (1839-1892). Woodblock print. Gift of Dr. and Mrs. Morris Shumiatcher, AGGV 2001.020.002*

COURTESANS PARADING ALONG THE FLOWER
PATH ROAD OF THE NEW YOSHIWARA DISTRICT.
Kunimasa IV (1848-1920). Woodblock print.
Gift of Philip Steel, AGGV 2003.020.001

* Note that some courtesans are experimenting with wearing Western dresses.

men, providing a beautiful and sensuous fantasy that all men desired. The geisha community came to be referred to as *karyukai* (the flower and willow world). Geisha were extensively trained in the traditional Japanese arts, many of which, such as poetry and music, were those of the aristocratic women of the imperial court. It was because of these glamorous women that much of the richness of traditional art and entertainment survived into modern Japan. Geisha became Japan's unparalleled conservators of traditional costume, music, singing, and dancing.

In the old days, the geisha were considered a city's valued possession and a measure of its vitality. Print artists of the Edo period portrayed the picturesque streets of the pleasure quarters and the women who inhabited them in *ukiyo-e* (pictures of the floating world). The beauties depicted in these woodblock prints were chiefly geisha and courtesans, not low-class prostitutes. Not only were geisha illustrated in prints; they were also celebrated in romantic novels and Kabuki plays and even gossiped about like celebrities in the newspapers that appeared in the nineteenth century.

The real life of the geisha was undoubtedly less appealing than her image. In Japan during the Edo period and even later, it was quite normal for large, poor families, especially in the countryside, to sell one or more of their daughters for money to support the family and reduce the number of mouths to feed. This practice was looked upon as a noble act: the girls were considered virtuous for "sacrificing themselves" so that the other members of the family could survive. It was the Confucian ideal of filial piety to fulfill a moral obligation and a family duty. Some families felt that, by selling their daughters to geisha households, they were giving them a chance to escape poverty and possible starvation and to have a better life, a good education, decent food, and the opportunity to wear beautiful clothing and to meet important people.

Clever, talented, and beautiful girls as young as six were sold to geisha households (*okiya*). Within those households, they became part of a new family composed entirely of women. Rigorously trained and subjected to often harsh discipline, they were expected to remain in servitude and not to try to escape. They were expected to endure and even to lose touch with their own emotions. This conflict between duty and human feeling (*giri* versus *ninjo*) became part of the geisha's life, in which she was expected not to fall in love. Despite the harshness of geisha life, it would generally have been better than being sent to a common brothel.

Geisha developed a rigidly structured hierarchical system with relationships based on the family or kin system, using the terms "mother/daughter" and "younger/older sister." This sisterhood was very important to survival in geisha society. It was a tying together of destinies (*sansan kudo*). Each girl had a senior, more experienced sister who helped in her training, passing down the traditional knowledge and strict etiquette. Within each household, there was a mother (*okasan*) who was in charge of the teahouse and who had to be an accomplished entrepreneur.

All girls started at the bottom, as maids (*shikomi*), but once they showed some promise of talent, they graduated to apprentice geisha (*maiko*). They began learning the geisha way of singing, dancing, playing musical instruments, and all the other skills their future profession would demand, such as flower arranging, participation in the tea ceremony, reading, and writing beautiful calligraphy. When these young women became full geisha, they were bound by contract and they owed the geisha household for their training, food and lodging, medical bills, and fabulous wardrobes and accessories. Some unscrupulous owners of geisha houses would try to reap even greater profits from their investment by overcharging her for everything, but even without that, the new geisha was enormously in debt.

Geisha learned to play the *kodaiko* (a small drum played with wooden sticks), the *tsuzumi* (a small drum played on the shoulder), and the *shamisen* (a three-stringed, banjolike instrument). The shamisen, played with a spatula-shaped piece of ivory or wood that is held in the hand, was the most important musical instrument, and it became an extension of the geisha's persona. Shamisen music, played only as an accompaniment to the human voice, was perfect for coaxing tone-deaf customers to sing along in their wavering voices. Trainees had to learn the music entirely by ear; some practiced the shamisen until their fingers bled. The training for singing and dancing was equally rigid. The dances (*nihon buyo* or *jiutamai*) were much-revered geisha arts, partly derived from the No and Kabuki theaters. Most geisha became highly competent musicians, singers, and dancers, attaining a deep and far-ranging knowledge of a number of styles of dance and music.

Not only did the maiko have to spend hours perfecting the finer details of her artistic pursuits; she also was trained in courtly mannerisms and social etiquette and was required to learn an archaic geisha vocabulary. She had to know how to walk, sit, and speak according to certain rules of the geisha world. She learned how to dress in layers of lavish silks, elegantly but with flair. She accompanied her experienced "older sister" on her appointed rounds to the teahouses and parties, to become familiar with the routine and in the hope that she would gain recognition among the customers when she became a geisha. Her costume was more formal than that of a

COURTESAN
Kikugawa Eizan
(1787–1867)
Hanging scroll, ink
and colors on silk
Gift of Mary Hummel,
AGGV 90.26.1

14

full geisha and she wore her hair and kimono differently. The maiko had to learn how to sleep on a lacquered wooden pillow, or *takamakura*—padded to ease her neck—so that her hairdo would not get mussed. When she became a geisha she would wear a wig and no longer have to sleep so uncomfortably.

The geisha's movements expressed romance and eroticism. She had to know how to flatter, to flirt, and to please men. Witty and clever conversation was her prime asset, prized more highly than her beauty—or at least that is what Japanese men claimed to appreciate the most in a geisha. Little has been written about the geisha's erotic or amorous skills, but no doubt she learned a great deal about sex from the "pillow books" (*makura-e*) provided as part of her education. The explicitly erotic images in these books of woodblock prints (called *shunga*—spring picture—or *higa*—secret pictures) served as sex education manuals for women and men in old Japan. The apprentice geisha was considered a stylized vision of an unblemished virgin girl. Her sexual initiation was part of becoming a full geisha. In the past, customers

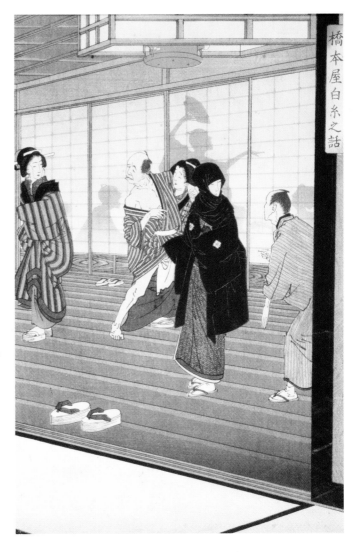

COURTESAN SHIRAITO OF THE TEAHOUSE HASHIMOTO-YA. *Taiso Yoshitoshi (1839–1892). Woodblock print, part of a diptych. Gift of Richard Steel, AGGV 85.6.3*

paid large sums of money for the privilege of deflowering a maiko in a ceremony called *mizu-age*, which typically took place when the girl had reached seventeen to nineteen years of age. After the defloration, the maiko would change the color of her kimono's collar from red to white, signifying that she had given up her virginity.

With her perfect balance of beauty, knowledge of the arts, and cultivated etiquette, the geisha became a living work of art. Her greatest expense lay in keeping up her kimono wardrobe. When she began her career, she was obliged to purchase at least ten kimono, and the garments would continue to be a burden on her budget throughout her working life. She needed a large number of them since she had to have the right kimono for the right place, the right season, and the right occasion. If an evening event or party went on too late, she would change into another kimono. From the late eighteenth century to the early twentieth century, the geisha were fashion trendsetters. Their gorgeous costumes and elegant mannerisms exuded avant-garde style (*iki*). Geisha would often vie with each other for originality and novelty of display in their dress. They knew how to parade their kimono with a flash of "pale" at the sleeve and below the hem of the kimono, a collar pulled down, a train on the ground, and the kimono's skirt held gracefully in the left hand. The celebrities and supermodels of their time, geisha were the primary arbiters of kimono fashion. The geisha became an emblem of Japan and the ideal of Japanese femininity.

The geisha also incurred major expenses for hairstyling and makeup. Her elaborate wigs, designed and constructed by specialists to suit the shape of her head, required several fittings and professional monthly combing and resetting.

A milk-white complexion has been a symbol of womanly beauty in Japan since the Heian period (794–1185). The geisha's facial makeup included a powdered white foundation with a slight accent at the eyes and starkly painted red lips. For extra sensual appeal, a red streak might be painted at the nape of the neck, on an otherwise unpainted area.

Geisha enjoyed the company of patrons (*danna*) who had iki—style—and who were willing to spend money freely. If a geisha was clever and lucky, she might be able to extract herself from her indenture by finding a patron who would pay off her debts and make her his mistress. With her costly kimono and accessory requirements, the geisha was the ultimate luxury item. The danna might buy his geisha mistress a teahouse or restaurant, and perhaps provide for her in his will.

Geisha won the trust and affection of men of intellect—actors, poets, and artists—and men of power, such as samurai, generals, captains of industry, entrepreneurs, cabinet ministers, and aristocrats—even men of the imperial household. Some of the nation's most important business took place with geisha present; ideas were freely discussed, deals were made, wars planned, and plots hatched. These men knew they could depend on the geisha's code of silence to keep her from divulging anything she overheard. Her livelihood depended upon total discretion and confidentiality, and her secrecy and mystery were part of her erotic appeal.

The Japanese tradition of arranged marriages precluded romantic interests within them; husbands turned instead to the geisha. Wives were considered sober, serious, and modest, while geisha were witty, artistic, and risqué. Until relatively recently, a wealthy Japanese man rarely appeared in public with his wife and seldom, if ever, brought business colleagues to his home to socialize. It was the geisha who was trained and equipped to perform the role of hostess; thus she was a key component of evening activities at society's top level. Knowing one's way around the geisha teahouses and being acquainted with well-known geisha were important social and business assets for an ambitious executive.

The Meiji period (1868–1912) was a golden age for the geisha (especially the prosperous 1890s). Japan underwent a remarkable transformation from a feudal state to a modern industrial, military, and political power during the Meiji period. The Meiji government enthusiastically imitated Western ways in politics, the military, education, industry, transportation, communications, and architecture. Modernization became synonymous with Westernization, and it resulted in Japan's winning major wars with China (1894–1895) and Russia (1904–1905).

However, a strong backlash came from adherents to traditional Japanese ways. Nationalists denounced attempts to imitate the West as insults to the national character. They made sport of the indiscriminate haste to look and behave like Westerners and held up the geisha as the guardians of the old Japanese traditions. Some geisha had tried to keep up with the times by experimenting with Western clothes and getting Western hairdos, but then they didn't seem like geisha anymore. By the 1930s they stopped trying to be mainstream fashion innovators, went back to wearing the kimono, and settled into their new role as curators of tradition by working to preserve the classic arts and dress.

During the Taisho period (1912–1926), Japan's great industrial development produced a working class in the big cities. Education stimulated a popular desire to participate in political affairs.

There were great hopes for the future and for political democracy, but economic problems in Japan in the 1920s and the worldwide depression of the 1930s ended those dreams. Militarism and an aggressive expansionist foreign policy took shape.

With new competition from café girls, geisha teahouses and restaurants began losing money. Geisha were briefly popular again just before World War II, as anti-Western and nationalistic fervor flourished and the geisha were considered uniquely Japanese. They continued to cater to their clients until 1944, when geisha restaurants were shut down and many geisha were put to work in war-related factories while others fled to the countryside. After the war the geisha returned to the cities, little by little, to resume their trade. Laws passed in 1947 pushing up compulsory education to the age of fifteen undermined the geisha profession. Since a young girl was now prohibited from becoming a maiko until she was fifteen, her important years of early training were eliminated.

The Anti-Prostitution Law of 1956 left the geisha unaffected, but by the late twentieth century, geisha began to lose their appeal and glamour. They seemed dull, too steeped in tradition, too expensive, too conservative, frozen in time. Geisha had become an anachronism, chiefly popular only with old or nostalgic men; young men of style and sophistication no longer wished to be seen with them. By clinging to the old ways, the geisha had now ensured their own demise, becoming a relic of the past.

HEAD OF A COURTESAN, *Kitagawa Utamaro (1753-1806). Woodblock print. Gift of Misses A. and K. McEwan, AGGV 950.007.001*

THE GEISHA ICHIMARU
*Kiyoshi Kobayakawa
(1898–1948). Woodblock
print. Given in memory of
Mrs. Theo Wiggan by her
Ikebana students and friends,
AGGV 2001.019.001*

In 1932, the prominent
Shin Hanga (New Print
Movement) artist Kiyoshi
Kobayakawa met Ichimaru
and became infatuated with
her. He produced both a
magnificent painting and a
popular and award-winning
woodblock print of her.

Born near the end of the prosperous Meiji period, Ichimaru was a teenager in the 1920s, when the economy's agricultural sector failed and much of Japan's rural population faced famine and massive unemployment. Once again, desperate families sold children into brothels. Home Ministry documents show that in six prefectures of northeastern Japan, sixty thousand girls were sold into slavery in 1934 alone. The lucky ones were sold to geisha houses, but most went to brothels or became slaves of restaurant owners who forced them into prostitution. This was the historical situation that Ichimaru experienced in her first thirty years. Her life would then encompass the military occupation of parts of China and elsewhere in Asia during the Second World War, followed by her country's devastation, and in turn followed by a remarkable national rebuilding.

Ichimaru was born into poverty in Nakatsugawa, Gifu Prefecture, on July 16, 1906, with the birth name of Mitsue Goto. Her parents had eleven children, ten of whom were girls. The youngest child, a boy, died at an early age. There were too many mouths to feed, and Ichimaru had to leave home to work in a geisha house at the age of fourteen or fifteen. Because of the confidentiality of geisha, little is known of Ichimaru's early life in the profession. Though she never spoke of her parents, she never forgot her early childhood and the hardships she faced growing up in small, remote Nakatsugawa. One of her record album jackets bears the assertion that "Proceeds of the sale of this record will go to the improvement of educational facilities for children in remote regions."

Ichimaru started out working as a low-ranking geisha or *oshaku*-waitress (one who serves sake) at a hot-spring spa in Nagano Prefecture. Groups of businessmen or friends came to such spas to get drunk and to enjoy geisha and bar girls. The geisha of these hot-spring resorts had a rather poor reputation and were not known for their performing arts, but Ichimaru became determined to improve her skills. She left for Tokyo, where her singing caught the ear of the Fujita Restaurant's proprietress. At the age of nineteen, Ichimaru was accepted by Ichimatsu-ya, a geisha house whose master was a noted actor at the Miyato Theater. Mitsue Goto took the name Asakusa Ichimaru in 1926; she would later drop "Asakusa" and be simply known as Ichimaru. (Many geisha had names that began with the character pronounced *ichi,* representing a tie with a particular branch of geisha.) Asakusa was one of the geisha quarters of Tokyo, which was known for its high and strict standards of training in the artistic pursuits of the geisha. During Ichimaru's years as a Tokyo geisha, from

1926 to 1933, the geisha—beset by competition from café girls—decided to abjure Western ways and continue as companions to men who would appreciate traditional Japanese talents.

Determined to make herself stand out from other geisha, Ichimaru took shamisen and singing lessons, *kiyomoto* style, from the famous female shamisen artist-teacher and authority, Enchiga Kiyomoto. The outstanding teacher helped Ichimaru to become a highly skilled shamisen artist, especially in the music of the old Edo period to which she devoted herself. Ichimaru further enhanced her skills by training under Grand Head Master Enjudaiyu Kiyomoto V's son, Eijudaiyu. She came to enjoy a reputation as the geisha who possessed a singing voice "like a nightingale," elegant good looks, and consummate skill with the shamisen. Ichimaru often appeared at the first-class inn-restaurant Kinsen

(Golden Fountain). Her talent was in great demand not only in the teahouses and restaurants of the Asakusa geisha district, to which she belonged, but also at the top-flight restaurants of the other geisha districts.

In the late 1920s and early 1930s, radio broadcasts and records began to replace stage, teahouse, and street performances. Several recording companies competed to attract talent; their agents searched the pleasure districts, scouting for talented geisha. Victor Recording company, established in 1927, discovered two remarkably talented geisha, Katsutaro and Ichimaru, and signed them to exclusive contracts in 1931. That year, to promote an amusement park in Shizuoka

Prefecture, the famous poet Kitahara Hakushu was commissioned to write the lyrics for a song, "Chakkiri Bushi (Tea-Picking Song)," set to music written by Machida Kasei. This unique contemporary folk song was chosen for Ichimaru's first record.

Katsutaro and Ichimaru, with their contrasting singing styles, immediately became rivals under the Victor label. Katsutaro had a cheerful, high-pitched voice, while Ichimaru sang in a low, crisp, and coquettish voice. Their rivalry resulted in a flowering of popular traditional songs in Japan. Ichimaru's popularity continued to rise; eventually her hits outstripped those of Katsutaro.

In 1933 Ichimaru recorded a song for the movie *Wet Swallow* (*Nure Tsubame*) that became a major hit. Her rendition of "Down the Tenryu River (Tenryu Kudareba)" elevated Ichimaru's position to that of superstar status. Praise from the composer Shinpei Nakayama for her performance of the song encouraged

23

Ichimaru to give up her life as a geisha to become a full-time recording artist. "Tenryu Kudareba" and another song she recorded, "Ryukyo Ko-Uta," were both folk songs of Nagano, and they helped to turn the mountainous region into an important tourist destination. The songs' lyrics, which commemorate Nagano's famous cherry blossoms, are now engraved on a stone monument at the Tenryu River gorge.

During Japan's expansionist wars in Manchuria and China in the 1930s, Ichimaru was called upon to perform for war factory workers and for troops, both at home and abroad. She was used to entertaining in relatively small and intimate places such as the dining rooms of inn-restaurants, but

now she was performing on large stages in front of huge audiences. She had to change her performance style to fit the situation, and the change became a turning point in her career. Her refined movements gave way to bigger, more expressive gestures.

In 1940, Ichimaru recorded more new songs, written by top songwriters and composers of traditional Japanese music. She courted famous poets and composers, inviting them to her home in Yanagibashi. But after the full-scale war with the United States began in late 1941, she recorded less frequently, stopping altogether between 1944 and 1948. In 1949 she established her radio program, *Mitsukoshi Calendar of Songs*; the show would last for ten years.

Ichimaru's strength lay in her tremendous adaptability. During the gloomy and chaotic postwar years of American military occupation, traditional Japanese popular songs were replaced by music to suit the tastes of the American GI.

A popular jazz singer of the time, Shizuko Kasagi, had become famous for her boogies. Ichimaru asked Ryoichi Hattori, the most popular composer of boogies, to write a song for her, the now well-known "Shamisen Boogie Woogie." Wearing her kimono and her geisha-style coiffure, Ichimaru sang and danced "Shamisen Boogie Woogie," "Snow Blues," and "Shamisen Waltz."

Ichimaru was the first Japanese singer to be invited to perform in Hawaii after the war, in 1950. The following year, she was invited to perform for the Japanese community in Brazil. She also sang for Kabuki theater performances and composed her own *Ko-uta* songs, which showed her talent at expressing emotion in her music; her style came to be known as "Ichimaru Air." She always performed with her shamisen accompanist, her sister Shizuko, who played along even if there was an orchestra.

With the arrival of television in Japan in the late 1950s, Ichimaru became a popular guest on national TV; she would remain in demand as a guest for more than twenty years. Critics called her a "great and unparalleled singer." From the 1960s through into the 1990s, Ichimaru received frequent honorific titles and awards, including honors from the Nakamura Kabuki School, NHK Radio/TV, and the government.

Ichimaru continued to teach and perform well into old age. But by 1997, when she passed away at the age of ninety-one, most of her money was gone. Throughout her life, her sisters regularly requested loans and she generously gave them money; near the end of her life her housekeeper walked off with much of her fortune, thought to be as much as 80 million yen. Ichimaru did, however, leave behind a tremendous legacy to Japanese music. Her triumph over adversity in becoming an outstanding, internationally known diva, is a remarkable story.

Ichimaru's collection of fine silk kimono includes a wide range of superb designs, some traditional, some very modern. The term *kimono* (from *mono,* thing, and *kiru,* to wear) came into use in the Meiji period, when the fad for all things Western led to a need to distinguish between Japanese and European clothing. It has come to mean the T-shaped outer garment based on the *kosode* (small sleeves), the outer garment of the urban elite of the Edo period. From the late sixteenth through the mid-nineteenth century, the Momoyama and Edo periods, the kosode became not just a garment but a work of art. Its structure, and the social and economic developments of the times, encouraged the decoration of its surface by artists and artisans.

The kimono is made from full widths of the bolt of kimono fabric, about 35 centimeters (13³/₄ inches) wide, sewn with a simple running stitch, wrapped around the body, and tied at the waist with a sash. The length of a kimono bolt is 11 to 11.4 meters (36 to 37 feet), enough to make one adult-size kimono. Until quite recently, kimono were never ready-made: a customer chose her bolt of fabric and had the garment made to measure. Two straight lengths of fabric, sewn up the middle in the back and left open over the shoulders and down the front, make the body of the kimono. A half-length section is sewn to each side in the front to form an overlap, left over right, and sleeves, each another width of the fabric, are attached to the sides of the body. A neckband or collar is attached to the neckline and extended about a third of the way down the front opening. For a heavy customer, the entire width of the bolt may be needed to form the kimono's body. For a thin one, none of the width of the fabric is trimmed off; it is simply folded into the seams at the side. The kimono is not tailored to a specific length for each customer: excess length is bloused over a hidden cord at the hips and held by the obi (sash) so that the garment's hem is kept from touching the ground.

A kimono to be cleaned is taken apart; then the lengths are sewn back together to form a strip of fabric of the original bolt length. This is washed and stretched over bamboo supports to dry. One of Ichimaru's kimono, a bush clover (*hagi*) pattern on a greenish silk crepe, which she is shown wearing on one of her record album covers, is in that strip form for washing. Since the fabric strips forming the kimono are not cut and shaped as in Western clothing, the kimono presents an ideal canvas for the textile artist. Individual style in dress is shown in the kimono not by cut and construction and shapes but by the choice of surface decoration: color, texture, pictorial design, and various decorative techniques. Although the shape of kimono does not change, Japanese who are educated in kimono fashion are able to identify whether a particular kimono is trendy or old-fashioned. Today top-level designer-craftspeople of kimono fabric are artists who have been trained not only in dyeing techniques but also in painting and graphic art at the university and art school level. Their works show the influence of contemporary art movements in Japan and abroad.

Until the end of the sixteenth century, silk from China was the preferred fabric for fine kimono. With the support of the warlord Toyotomi Hideyoshi (1536–1598), the native Japanese silk industry came alive and Kyoto became a center of quality silk production. At first the decoration was primarily in the weave, with sumptuous brocades, and in the embroidery, which often suggested brocade designs but then began to develop in a pictorial style of its own. Other, often very expensive, forms of decoration included tie-dye and stencil; the latter frequently featured gold and silver leaf and powder (*surihaku*). Silk could be painted, and fine artists such as Ogata Korin, Matsumura Goshun, and Gion Nankai decorated kimonos. Government sumptuary laws, attempting especially to restrict the display of wealth by everyday townspeople, encouraged the development of new textile decoration techniques.

An important approach to decoration, and one that is well represented by the kimono shown in this book, is the paste-resist dyeing technique called *yuzen*, after the Kyoto artist-monk Miyazaki Yuzen (active late seventeenth–early eighteenth century). The yuzen process combined old and new traditions and quickly became very popular. Miyazaki Yuzen was known for decorating fans with classical literary themes; yuzen kimono designs are noted for expressing themes from classical Japanese poems and novels and from traditional sayings.

In the lengthy yuzen process, outlines of the designs are drawn on the fabric; then a line of starch paste or glue is applied to the drawing from a cloth tube with a metal tip, like a cake-decorating tube. Once the paste has dried, dyes of various colors are brushed on within the starch boundaries, which prevent the bleeding of one color into another. The fabric is steamed to set the dyes, then the starch paste is washed away in cold water (the workman had to stand waist deep in cold running water for this part of the process). The designs are covered with a protective glue-paste, which in turn is coated with sawdust, and the background is brush-dyed. The fabric is steamed again, then rinsed in cold water and given a final steaming to stretch and smooth it. Further decoration, if any—embroidery or silver or gold leaf—may now be done.

The yuzen process was developed over a long period, with many changes. Overall background coloring became much easier with the introduction of synthetic dyes to Japan about 1862. Some natural dyes, such as indigo, required immersion dyeing, a process which required complex and painstaking craftsmanship, in combination with yuzen dyeing. Synthetic dyes could be brush-painted on, evenly, for the background, allowing a more colorful effect and making yuzen kimono both more popular and more cheaply available to the general public. The shift of decoration to the lower part of the kimono's skirt in the late nineteenth century, which left a much larger plain area, was not only a reaction against earlier overly decorated kimono and a result of the influence of the ever-widening obi but also a design that would have reduced the cost of production. This change was facilitated by the ease of brushing on the synthetic dyes. Techniques of re-pasting and re-dyeing to hide the white outline left by paste reserves were developed; and in the twentieth century, dye-infused pastes were also applied through stencils, leaving the dye in the fabric once the paste was washed out. Nakamura Katsuma (1894–1982) was one of the first artist/artisans to receive recognition as a "Possessor of Important Intangible Cultural Assets" for working with the *musenfuse* (no-line-resist) technique of drawing directly on the fabric; yuzen dyers had until then considered musenfuse a lower-class technique.

Two major centers, Kyoto and Kanazawa, are famous for yuzen dyeing. Most of Ichimaru's kimono were made to order by the Mitsukoshi Department Store of Tokyo. Mitsukoshi, like Harrods of London, is an old establishment, known for quality merchandise, that caters to high-society customers. The store has always ordered its yuzen-dyed kimono fabric from Kyoto.

In the early Meiji period, from 1868 into the 1880s, fascination with the West almost led to the abandonment by the elite of Japanese traditions, including Japanese-style clothing. The reaction in the 1890s against the abandonment of Japanese culture did bring back the kimono, but now it was worn chiefly by women. (It had been worn by both sexes and by all classes and ages until the Meiji period. By the end of the twentieth century, however, women too had largely stopped wearing the kimono, except for a few special or ceremonial occasions, such as weddings.)

The style of kimono and the way they were worn during the twentieth century is based on the rather stiff and formal nineteenth-century tradition of the samurai class. In the twentieth century, all the nuances of kimono wearing were carefully studied and the rules of etiquette closely followed. The kimono types have been precisely ranked as to formality and style, as follows:

FURISODE (long swinging sleeves): This is the most formal style, for a young, unmarried girl; it is often brightly colored or highly decorated, and its sleeves reach to the calf or ankle.

TOMESODE (clipped sleeves): Worn by a married woman or any woman over twenty-two years old, and suitable for most formal occasions, the tomesode will be black or white, with five crests on the shoulders and any other decoration primarily in the area along the hem and lower front edges (*tsuma moyo*) or concentrated along the hem (*susomoyo*). For less formal occasions, the tomesode will have three crests and may be in other colors with tsuma moyo or susomoyo decoration.

HOMONGI (visiting wear): Worn for semiformal visits and parties, it has no crests; decoration is allowed on shoulders and sleeves as well as on the body of the robe.

YUKATA: An unlined cotton kimono worn in summer for errands and casual occasions.

Other garment types include:

UCHIKAKE: A highly decorated kimono with a padded hem for a train, formerly worn loose and unbelted over all other robes, on formal or ceremonial occasions; it is now worn only as a bridal gown. The bridal uchikake has long swinging sleeves (furisode).

JUBAN or NAGAJUBAN: An underkimono.

HAORI: A jacketlike outer garment worn over the kimono. The front edges hang parallel rather than overlapping.

OBI: The sash worn to hold the kimono closed and enhance its beauty is carefully selected to blend or contrast with the kimono. The obi's length is about three meters and its width about twenty-five centimeters. There are nearly twenty different ways to tie it, but the *otaiko* (drum) style was most often used.

Most twentieth-century Japanese who wore the kimono did so with stiff formality. The exceptions were the geisha. At the turn of the past century, geisha had considerable status in Japan, largely due to their support of the samurai who overthrew the Tokugawa shogunate. Geisha also continued the Edo tradition of style or chic (iki) and wore their kimono with great panache—open, sweeping behind them with padded hems, often with dramatic patterns or color combinations. The difference in the way a geisha and a non-geisha dressed is easily evident to the initiate's eye. The nape of the neck and the upper part of the geisha's body are more exposed, and there is a looseness about her neckband, but in spite of this she looks neat and tidy. The geisha may wear any type of kimono, from the furisode to the five-crested tomesode, and she chooses the one best suited to the song or dance she performs.

Ichimaru continued the geisha tradition of dressing with style and elegance when she became a popular singer. Her kimono collection includes many with traditional motifs, including seasonal or classical literary themes, and their design and rendition show that in the twentieth century, kimonos continued to be works of art.

市丸

Japanese terms used in kimono making

CHIRIMEN *silk crepe*

KOMA-NUI *couching*

MON *crest*

RINZU *damask-like figured silk satin*

RO *silk gauze*

SHIBORI *tie-dyeing*

SURIHAKU *gold or silver leaf or powder decoration*

YUZEN *paste-resist dyeing*

TOMESODE WITH PINES AND CLOUDS AND FIVE NAKAMURA FAMILY CRESTS
Paste-resist dyeing; gold embroidery and stenciling; silk crepe

Its formal style, with the pine tree motif (pine branches are a New Year's symbol), would make this kimono appropriate for ceremonial occasions associated with New Year's. Ichimaru revived the Edo-style popular song with the chanting style of singing of the Kabuki theater, and especially of the Nakamura School of Kabuki. In gratitude, the Nakamura School bestowed on her the title of headmistress of Edo-style vocal training in the Nakamura Performing Arts School, allowing her to use the Nakamura family crest, a stylized ginkgo leaf within a watchtower outline.

TOMESODE WITH CRANES AND CLOUDS AND FIVE *TACHIBANA* (TANGERINE FLOWER) CRESTS
Paste-resist dyeing; gold leaf and gold powder stenciling; silk crepe

The black color, five crests, and padded hem indicate that Ichimaru would have worn this kimono for formal dancing or singing. The design of the crane, an auspicious symbol associated with long life, is carried onto the inside of the kimono, where it would have been seen as Ichimaru held the garment up to move.

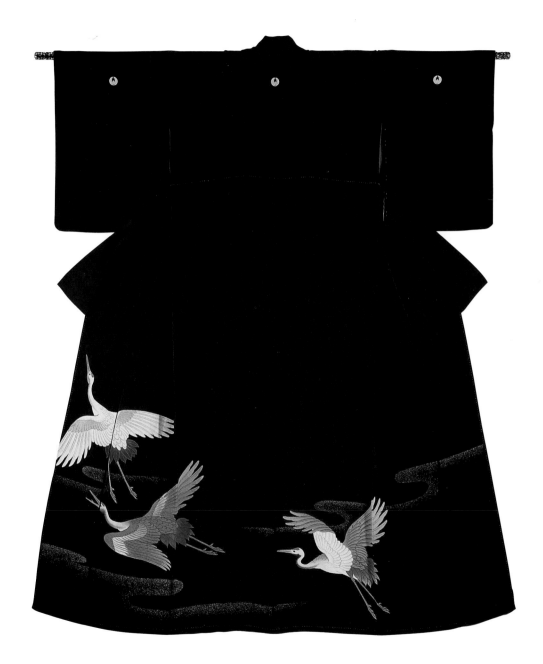

HOMONGI WITH TREES AND UNIDENTIFIED ARTIST'S SEAL, "TEI"
Paste-resist dyeing; gold thread embroidery; silk crepe

The lining and underlayer are in a "powdered-tea color," according to the storage wrapper. The embroidery is very fine, with couched stitches (cross stitches holding laid-on lines of thread in place) and shading created by variation in stitch density.

HOMONGI WITH PEACOCKS AND SCATTERED PEACOCK FEATHERS
Paste-resist dyeing; gold and colored silk thread embroidery; silk crepe

This is a superb example of yuzen dyeing and embroidery. The embroidery stitches on the blue-and-green peacock's head become sparser the farther down the neck, with the last part of the neck represented only by a dyed pattern. This gives the bird a strongly three-dimensional effect. Peacocks are considered auspicious, but they are somewhat rare as kimono motifs. In the 1930s the Kyoto fabric artist Minagawa Gekka (1892–1987) produced an Art Deco–style kimono fabric with dyed peacocks and flowers; it was made into a spectacular uchikake, which was exhibited at the Kyoto Municipal Museum of Art in 1988.

HOMONGI WITH SCENE OF YANAGIBASHI
Paste-resist dyeing; silver stenciling; silk crepe

The bridge and riverbank depicted in black above a blue area of water with silver clouds represents Yanagibashi (Willow Bridge), the Tokyo geisha quarter where Ichimaru lived and worked. The branches on the kimono's shoulders are those of the willow tree. Ichimaru wears this kimono in the photograph on one of her record album covers.

43

TOMESODE WITH CHRYSANTHEMUM BLOSSOMS AND THREE TACHIBANA CRESTS
Silk embroidery; damask-like figured silk satin

The silk has an overall pattern of paulownia blossoms in the weave. Chrysanthemums are associated with autumn. The form of the tachibana crest is different from that found on most of the other kimono, but all family crests have variant forms.

45

HOMONGI WITH BRANCH DESIGN AND UNIDENTIFIED ARTIST'S SEAL, "TEI"
Paste-resist dyeing; gold and silver embroidery; silk crepe

This purple (*fuji-iro*) kimono is another tour de force of dyeing technique. The decoration is known as "majolica" for the amazing variation in color and shading in the branches created through the yuzen dyeing process.

HOMONGI WITH CHRYSANTHEMUM BLOSSOMS
Paste-resist dyeing; gold and silver embroidery; silk crepe

Subtle gold rectangles were created by widely spaced parallel lines of gold thread laid down and then couched with brown cross-stitches, contrasting effectively with the flowers, done with tightly laid and couched heavy gold and silver thread.

HOMONGI WITH FIR TREES AND UNIDENTIFIED SEAL, AND MATCHING OBI

Paste-resist dyeing; gold stenciling; gold, silver, and rainbow-colored silk thread embroidery; silk crepe

The silk crepe's textured rough-smooth pattern is created by a special chirimen-weaving technique. The fir tree is a traditional symbol of winter. There is a matching obi in Tsuzure weave from Nishijin, Kyoto, where 90 percent of all obi are produced. If the motif designs on an obi are complex, it can take a month to weave only centimeters; such obi are very expensive.

TOMESODE WITH NANDINA BRANCHES AND THREE TACHIBANA CRESTS
Paste-resist dyeing; gold and orange silk thread embroidery; damask-like figured silk satin

The nandina plant is a symbol of the New Year, and this is an *awase*, or lined, winter-weight kimono: Ichimaru probably wore it for occasions associated with New Year's. The false edging between the acid green kimono and the white silk lining is a rust orange that echoes the color of the nandina berries, with a raised pattern of grasses in the weave.

TOMESODE WITH STYLIZED GEESE AND THREE TACHIBANA CRESTS
Paste-resist dyeing; silk crepe

This kimono might have been designed for Ichimaru to wear when she sang the sad love song "Hagure Gan (Strayed Wild Goose)" in the Ko-uta Kabuki style. An inside lining, in a red-and-white geometric design based on a variation of the *hishi* (diamond shape), simulates an inner kimono, with an additional royal blue edging between the patterned lining and the outer cream-and-blue kimono. The bold color contrasts are very "geisha" and theatrical, and the simple, strong design of the bird motifs would have carried in the large theaters where Ichimaru was appearing in the 1950s, when this may have been made.

55

HOMONGI WITH FANS

Paste-resist dyeing; gold leaf stenciling; small touches of gold embroidery; silk crepe

Basic yuzen dyeing decorates this fully lined kimono, with a few accents of gold stenciling and gold thread couched with red. The flower motifs on the fans—plum, peony, chrysanthemum, and maple—are auspicious themes associated with the seasons. The fan, too, is a symbol of good omen and good fortune.

TOMESODE WITH CAMELLIAS AND THREE TACHIBANA CRESTS
Paste-resist dyeing; silk crepe

This is a very elegant kimono with padded hem and the decoration done entirely in yuzen dyeing. The camellias, a New Year's flower, are shown on the inside at the center opening as well as on the outside: they would be seen as the kimono was held slightly open during a performance.

HOMONGI WITH DESIGN DEPICTING KIMONO HANGING ON ROPES
Paste-resist dyeing; gold and silver stenciling; gold, silver, and rainbow thread embroidery; silk crepe

The decoration on this homongi is very bold and dramatic. Kimono swirl in the wind on the lower part of the robe, and cherry blossom petals in rainbow thread embroidery and stenciled gold and silver are scattered on the shoulders. The kimono shown on the inside left of the front opening carries across to the front right side. The motifs on the various kimono include iris, with the characters "spring wind," water flowers and a stylized water swirl, wisteria, swallows, mallets, grasses, and the characters "a thousand birds" and "flower wave" on a silver basket weave pattern. The complex motifs are associated with the theme song of the movie *Nure Tsubame (Wet Swallow),* one of Ichimaru's early hit songs in the early 1930s, rerecorded in 1968. The verse of the song starts with "Spring wind."

61

UCHIKAKE WITH PEONIES, PHOENIX BIRDS, PAULOWNIA, AND CHERRY BLOSSOMS
Gold and silk embroidery; damask-like figured white silk satin; gold leaf stenciling on partial lining of damask-like figured pink silk satin

The motifs on this bride's-style uchikake with furisode sleeves are all highly auspicious themes. The partial lining in pink rinzu, with an overall geometric "fence" (*higaki*) or latticework damask design, is further decorated with squares of gold leaf. This uchikake might have been worn for Ichimaru's song "Hanayome Tokyo (Tokyo Bride)," which she sang in 1931 and rerecorded as late as 1990.

HOMONGI WITH FLOWERS AND VINE LEAVES
Paste-resist dyeing; silk crepe

Ichimaru's hit song "Down the Tenryu River" makes reference to the Japanese tradition that vines, like ropes, symbolize the bond between man and woman. Vines can also symbolize a woman's unwillingness to give up her love. This unlined kimono in creamy white and indigo resembles a yukata, or casual boudoir kimono. It seems appropriate for Ichimaru to have worn it to perform "Sanosa," a song of a woman who regrets that her lover has left her. This kimono resembles the one Ichimaru wears on a video when she sings "Sanosa."

TOMESODE WITH DESIGN OF FABRIC SCREEN WITH ROPES AND CLOUDS AND FIVE TACHIBANA CRESTS
Paste-resist dyeing; silk embroidery; gold and silver leaf and powder stenciling; damask-like figured heavy silk

This is the most formal style, with decoration only on the lower level of the kimono and with five crests, but the background color is peach rather than the usual black or white. The fabric curtain screen depicted (only on the kimono's left side) is the type seen in handscrolls of the Heian period, such as those that depict *The Tale of Genji*. Clouds are created with gold leaf and gold powder stenciling. The ropes' superb embroidery turns from gold to mauve and gold to white, with Japanese knots for the tassels.

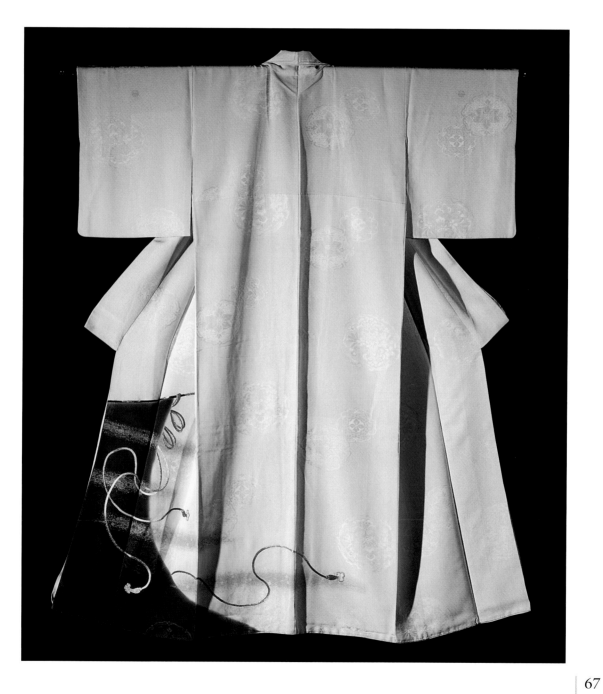

FURISODE WITH ABSTRACT GRAPEVINE PATTERN
Paste-resist dyeing; gold stenciling; silk crepe

The furisode is meant to be worn by a young woman, and the bold pattern and bright colors here are also appropriate to a young, unmarried woman. These rules were not followed by geisha, however, and even after she left the geisha profession to become a recording artist, Ichimaru followed geisha style. The motif of grapes and vines and exotic plants (*Budo karakusamoyo*) is as old as the Tempyo period (eighth century). Photographs show Ichimaru wearing this unlined summer kimono to perform in Hawaii in 1950, when she would have been in her forties. The kimono may have been made specifically for that performance, since it is poor-quality silk crepe and appears to have been made cheaply and quickly. At that time, Japanese textile and kimono manufacturers, like most businesses, had not recovered from World War II.

HOMONGI WITH FLUTES
Paste-resist dyeing; silk crepe

This is a lined winter kimono, although the season for wearing lined kimono actually lasts from September through May or June. The flute was one of the classical Japanese instruments played by geisha, but Ichimaru's instrument was the shamisen.

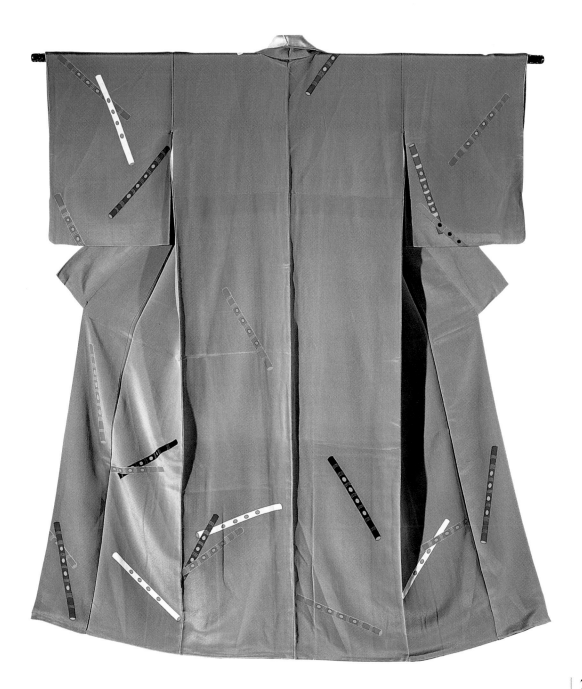

HOMONGI WITH LANDSCAPE SCENE OF ISLANDS WITH PINE TREES
Paste-resist dyeing; gold and colored thread embroidery; silk crepe

Pine-covered islands are a popular subject for the traditional Japanese woodblock print, ukiyo-e. The pale blue background aptly serves the purpose of both sky and ocean, with thin lines indicating waves.

HAORI (TWO EXAMPLES)
Paste-resist dyeing; silk gauze

The haori is a jacket that was worn in the Edo period by men, but around 1900 the most chic women, geisha especially, began to wear them. The haori was originally worn in winter, but the thin silk gauze of these haori indicates that they were worn in the summer. The autumn motifs are typical, however, since summer haori should suggest a touch of autumn cool.

A haori is made of two layers of silk gauze. The decorative motifs on the inner layer are seen clearly only when the haori is opened, but those motifs can be faintly glimpsed from the outside: a very subtle and elegant effect. The navy haori is decorated inside with Chinese bell flowers (*kikyo*) on a lattice. The black haori with tachibana crest is decorated inside with maple leaves.

DISASSEMBLED KIMONO

Bush clover pattern on silk crepe with gold thread

> This kimono has been sewn together in one long strip for laundering. It is interesting to note that the kimono is made of standardized strips that fit into one long panel.

WIG WITH CORAL HAIRPIN, USED BY ICHIMARU

BIBLIOGRAPHY

Cobb, Jodi. *Geisha: the Life, the Voices, the Art*. New York: Knopf, 1995

Dalby, Liza Crihfield. *Geisha*. Berkeley: University of California Press, 1983

——. *Kimono: Fashioning Culture*. New Haven, CT: Yale University Press, 1993

Deutsch, Sanna Saks and Link, Howard A. *The Feminine Image: Women of Japan*. Honolulu: Honolulu Academy of Arts, 1985

Downer, Lesley. *Geisha, The Secret History of a Vanishing World*. London: Headline, 2000

Gluckman, Dale Carolyn & Sharon Sadako Takeda. *When Art Became Fashion: Kosode in Edo-Period Japan*. New York: Weatherhill, 1992

Golden, Arthur. *Memoirs of a Geisha*. New York: Knopf, 1997

Ishimura Hayao et al. *Robes of Elegance: Japanese Kimonos of the 16th–20th Centuries*. Raleigh: North Carolina Museum of Art, 1988

Kennedy, Alan. *Japanese Costume, History and Tradition*. Paris: A. Biro, 1990

——. *Kosode, 16th–19th Century Textiles from the Nomura Collection*. Tokyo: Kodansha International, 1984

Liddell, Jill. *The Story of the Kimono*. New York: E. P. Dutton, 1989

Yang, Sunny and Rochelle M. Narasin. *Textile Art of Japan*. Tokyo: Shufunotomo/Japan Publications, 1989

JAPANESE REFERENCES

-*Nihon Bijutsu Zenshu (The Anthology of Japanese Art)*, Vol 21, pub. Gakken, 1979

-*Kimono no Subete (All About Kimono)* by Tadatsuka Ishizaki, pub. Tsuru Shobo, 1968

-*Kimono Bunkashi (Cultural History of Kimono)*, pub. The Asahi Shinbun Press, 1986

-*Kyo no Miyabi: Kinsei no Kyutei Bunka (Elegance of Kyoto: Imperial Court Culture of the Edo Period)*. Catalogue for the Exhibition, 1988

-*1930-nendai no Kyooto (Kyoto in the 1930s): Japanese-Style Painting, Western-Style Painting, and Crafts and Fabric Art*. Catalogue for the Exhibition, 1988

-*Ichimaru Hauta Meisaku-shu—okeiko-yo uta hon tsuki (Masterpieces of Ichimaru's Hauta-Songs—with texts for practice)*. Victor Music Book, MB-8502

-*Katei Gaho (Home Graphic Journal)*. Special New Year Edition, 1997, pub. Sekai Bunkasha